Tourist in Hell

ELEANOR WILNER

Tourist in Hell

THE UNIVERSITY OF CHICAGO PRESS
Chicago & London

ELEANOR WILNER is a former MacArthur Fellow and the author of seven collections of poetry, including *Otherwise* and *Sarah's Choice* (both published by the University of Chicago Press), and her most recent work, *The Girl with Bees in Her Hair* (2004).

The University of Chicago Press, Chicago 60637
The University of Chicago Press, Ltd., London
© 2010 by The University of Chicago
All rights reserved. Published 2010
Printed in the United States of America
19 18 17 16 15 14 13 12 11 10   1 2 3 4 5

ISBN-13: 978-0-226-90032-2 (paper)
ISBN-10: 0-226-90032-0 (paper)

Library of Congress Cataloging-in-Publication Data
Wilner, Eleanor.
    Tourist in hell / Eleanor Wilner.
        p. cm. —(Phoenix poets)
    Poems. Includes bibliographical references.
    ISBN-13: 978-0-226-90032-2 (pbk. : alk. paper)
    ISBN-10: 0-226-90032-0 (pbk. : alk. paper)
    I. Title. II. Series: Phoenix poets.
    PS3573.I45673T68 2010
    811'.54—dc22   2010012099

♾ The paper used in this publication meets the minimum requirements of the American National Standard for Information Sciences—Permanence of Paper for Printed Library Materials, ANSI Z39.48-1992.

to RICHARD A. MACKSEY,

who opened the way

Welcome. We're waiting for you, pretty lady.
What do you think hell is if it isn't history?

Hayden Carruth, "Tartar"

CONTENTS

Acknowledgments xiii

ONE

History as Crescent Moon 3
Opening the Eyes 4
Wreck and *rise above* 6
The Gyre 8
Geopolitics 10
In a Time of War 12
In That Dawn 14
After the Tsunami 16
What It Hinges On 18
Thinking about Unamuno's *San Manuel Bueno, Mártir* 19
Site Visit 20
Back Then, We Called It "The War" 22
The Show Must Go On 24
Magnificat 26

TWO

Establishment 31
Winter Lambs 33
Rendition, with Flag 35
Postcard with Statue of Liberty, No Message 36
Cold Dawn of the Day When Bush Was Elected for a
    Second Term 37
The Raven's Text 38
The meteor 39

High Noon 41
Saturday Night 42

THREE

Voices from the Labyrinth
- · Minos 49
- · Ariadne 50
- · Daedalus 52
- · The Minotaur 53

Meditation on DNA with Gene Splices from
 Shakespeare's Sonnets 55
An Ode to Asymmetry 58
To Think What We Might Have . . . 60
Four Flats, Getting Dark Soon, Nothing to Do but Walk 62
Like I really like that 64
Encounter in the Local Pub 66

FOUR

What loves, takes away 71
Restored to Blue 73
Vermeer's Girl, a Restoration 75
Trees, even at this distance 77
the palest flowers / ash, snow . . . 79
Larger to Those Who Stay 81

Welcome to the dollar bin 83
Meditation on Lines from Shakespeare's Sonnet 73 84
Harmony Bowl 86
Colony Collapse Disorder (CCD) 88
Such Stuff as Dreams Are Made On 90
The Morning After 92
Of a Word 94
Headlong for That Fair Target 96
Mine eyes have seen the glory of . . . 98
Tracking 100

Notes 101

ACKNOWLEDGMENTS

With thanks to the editors of the following publications in which these poems first appeared, occasionally in slightly altered forms and under different titles:

Boulevard: "Harmony Bowl," "Welcome to the dollar bin," and "Winter Lambs"

Cerise Press (online): "Colony Collapse Disorder (CCD)" and "Headlong for That Fair Target"

Cortland Review (online): "Vermeer's Girl, a Restoration," "Minos," "Ariadne," and "The Minotaur"

Front Porch, Texas State University (online): "What It Hinges On"

Kenyon Review: "Establishment," "An Ode to Asymmetry," and "Larger to Those Who Stay"

The Louisville Review: "Of a Word"

Maggid: "The Raven's Text"

Meena: "Postcard with Statue of Liberty, No Message"

Nightsun: "In a Time of War," "After the Tsunami" (originally "Afterwards"), *"the palest flowers / ash, snow . . . ,"* and "The Show Must Go On"

nor (*New Ohio Review*): "High Noon"

The Pedestal Magazine (online): "Of Such Stuff as Dreams Are Made On"

Per Contra (online): "The meteor"

Poetry: "History as Crescent Moon," "Magnificat," *"Wreck* and *rise above,"* "The Gyre," "Thinking about Unamuno's *San Manuel Bueno, Mártir,"* "To Think What We Might Have . . . ," "What loves, takes away," *"Mine eyes have seen the glory of . . . ,"* "Tracking," and "Encounter in the Local Pub"

Poetry International: "*Like I really like that*" and "Restored to Blue"
Poetry Northwest: "Meditation on DNA with Gene Splices from
    Shakespeare's Sonnets" and "Saturday Night"
Runes: "Back Then, We Called It 'The War'" (originally "Distress
    Signals in a Time of War") and "In That Dawn" (originally "But
    oh, to be young then . . .")
Sirena: "Four Flats, Getting Dark Soon, Nothing to Do but Walk"
Weber / The Contemporary West: "Geopolitics"

"Saturday Night" was reprinted in *Pushcart Prize XXXII: Best
    of the Small Presses 2008*, ed. Bill Henderson (Wainscott, NY:
    Pushcart Press, 2009); and in *Alhambra Poetry Calendar 2010*,
    ed. Shafiq Naz (Brussels: Alhambra Publishing, 2009).
"*Wreck* and *rise above*" was reprinted in *Alhambra Poetry Calendar
    2008*.
"*Mine eyes have seen the glory of . . .*" was reprinted in *Alhambra
    Poetry Calendar 2007*.
"History as Crescent Moon" was written for and appeared in a
    limited edition book, *The Inconstant Moon*, by book artist Enid
    Mark (Philadelphia: Elm Press, 2007).
The four poems titled "Voices from the Labyrinth: Minos, Ariadne,
    Daedalus, The Minotaur" were written for *Out of the Labyrinth*,
    by Enid Mark, to be published posthumously by Elm Press in a
    limited edition.

To Sam Hamill, to whom not just this writer but American poetry
owes a great debt. These poems owe thanks to all my friends, to the
students and faculty at the MFA Program for Writers at Warren
Wilson College for their inspired companionship, to my essential
readers Marcia Pelletiere and Heidy Steidlmayer, endless gratitude
to Denise Farran for the rescue, and to my amazing family: Bob,
Trudy, Mike, Noah, and Molly—without whom . . .

One

"Man learns from history that man learns nothing from history."

—Hegel

HISTORY AS CRESCENT MOON

The horns
   of a bull
      who was placed
before a mirror at the beginning
      of human time;
         in his fury
at the challenge of his double,
         he has, from
            that time to this,
been throwing himself against
            the mirror, until
            by now it is
shivered into millions of pieces—
            here an eye, there
            a hoof or a tuft
of hair; here a small wet shard made
            entirely of tears.
And up there, below the spilt milk of
            the stars, one
            silver splinter—
parenthesis at the close of a long sentence,
         new crescent,
      beside it, red
      asterisk of
   Mars
*

3

OPENING THE EYES

The dust of chiseled stone spackled
      the concrete floor, the sculptor all but finished
with his work. It stood, enormously, on a branch
      of darkly veined marble, its body cut
from a smooth and gleaming chunk of white
      that caught the light with such intensity
you felt a need to look away, as if to look
      too long would blind. Its feathers,
cut in sharp relief, catch the shadows;
      you can feel the power in its talons
as they grasp the sculpted branch. But
      the great eyes of the owl, black orbs
of obsidian, refuse the gaze—their blank
      and obdurate sheen mirrors only
what it does not see. The cooled
      volcanic glass gives back the sculptor's
face, so its indifference seems his own.
      The owl was to be his masterpiece—
he who had torn for years the living forms
      from rock, exposed its veins,
who found what granite hid or marble
      wore within; his owl would be
freed from the burden of bad augur,
      released back to the wild from history,
iconography, and from Athena—
      the armored, icy mind of war, what posed
as wisdom, but was policy.

Something was wrong with the eyes,
the great stone owl inanimate, inert,
        for all the care he'd lavished on its form,
its tensing on the branch, the slight lift of its wings.
        For hours he sat before it, unsatisfied, fury slowly
growing at the failure of his hands.
        Then all at once he burst from his chair,
and chisel in hand, attacked the black
        uncaring empty gaze. And as he split
the center of each eye, as if
        to make the pupil see the light,
        the owl cried out—heart-scalding shriek
        that tore the night: cried out
        for what it could not help
        but see.

WRECK AND *RISE ABOVE*

Because of the first, the fear of wreck,
which they taught us to fear (though we learned
at once, and easily),
                          because of the wreck
that was expected (and metal given velocity
and heft to assure it)—
                          we became adepts in
rise above: how many versions: the church
steeple that took the eye straight up to
heaven (though it seemed snagged on
the cross-beam of that cross, torn blue
at the top, where sense leaked out). And
rise above, transcendence, on that higher
plane, the vertical direction of virtue (a bony
finger pointing up to where matter dissolves
into distaste for it);
                          the space program, expensive
tons of rocket (soon to be debris) fired off
the planet's crust at anything out there, pocked
moon, red rocky Mars, *ever the upward
urge*, carved in the marble arch of the old library
door under which generations passed,
hoping to rise above it all—

6

like the woman the magician levitates
over the table, her body floating an unlikely
inch or two above the velvet-draped plateau . . .
watch her hovering, weightless,

                          the crowd staring
in wonder, the trick of the thing still hidden,
and the magician doing something now
with his hands, a flurry of brilliant
silk in the air, as she floats
in the endlessness of art,

                          the magician
still waving his scarves, the air a bright
shatter of wings, doves from a hat,
our disbelief suspended,
while below, the wrecks accumulate:
scrapyard, broken concrete slabs, and
all those bodies not exempt from gravity,
beneath our notice as we ride
above it all, like froth on a wave
that will be water falling by the ton,
soon, when the tide turns.

THE GYRE

The world was a globe that sat on a table
in a fire-lit study, the table covered
with a rich, tooled leather; while
the man who spun the globe—matching
countries with the map spread out below
on the desk from which he reached
an arm to turn the little effigy of world—
was shifting borders in his head, so that
the spinning orb began to glow
with his desire, his designs. As if his dreams
had given off a smoke, a thick fog
cloaked and altered everything he saw—

so even now, when all the corpses from that spin
have long since rotted in the grave,
the clouds have not dispersed, their swirling
smoke obscures all but the twisted steel
of a foregone conclusion, the world unmade,
as centuries and cities fall, cascade
into the landfill of history—worlds born
on the waste of those that came before.
As a glowing cloud of smoke will hang
over a burning dump at night, and the bears
and raccoons come out, eyes shining in the dark,
to paw through the smoldering heaps—

just so the historian sits, sifting and sifting
entrails, cornices, motives, bones—all
that is left to be indexed and filed,
rearranged, given syntax and sense;
above him, stuffed birds—a condor, a gull,
a carrion crow, moth-eaten by time,
look down on his labors
with a bright, glassy-eyed malice
from their dusty cases, and,
stirring a little on their perches, try
with beaks their walls of glass:
here and there now, hairline cracks,
and as night falls, the sound of taps.

GEOPOLITICS

Moon on the desert, a shimmer
in the wash, nearby the pack rat is drawn
to that pale, shifty light, his burrow
and its hoard (they comfort him)
left far below. But the glittering
light eludes him as he darts
off across the stony ground,
small charcoal stroke in search
of something bright; and the owl,
unmoving as the cactus arm,
has the greater need. Or, no,
the wing span, and the speed.

Like a note of ponderous brass
in a play of pipes and shadows,
the armadillo, laminated soul,
fresh from nature's cannery,
scuttles into view, makes his way
across the wash—a dry gully waiting
for rain . . . close by, the dark grumbles,
while further out, the planets burn
like signal fires across the vacancy,
their message our belittlement,
far beyond the scrubby sky that
mothers us, hovering, gray

with its worry of clouds.
The armadillo covers his own
back, and with long claws digs
furiously his tunnel in the hard
desert clay, fearing invasion,
and disappears into his own
armored dark, taking the stars
with him, as the horizon lightens
toward dawn, and the owl closes
his eyes, his mind filled
with the small, satisfactory
cries of the rat, his stomach
with the rat's debris.

IN A TIME OF WAR

Flies, caught in the sap of the living
tree, someday will be
precious, dressed in amber—just so
the past appears to the present, gem-
like in its perfect preservation,
the hardened gold of yesterday, a relic
through which today's sun shines.

But those who are caught in the sticky
sap of actual time, insects in the odds
against them, who struggle in the ooze,
slowly sink into the mass,
the numberless, anonymous dead . . .
till the atrocious becomes
the mundane, our senses numb
from the sheer litany of repetition.

Let us, then, just watch this one small
desperate fly, stuck first by the feet,
and then, in its struggles, entangled
entirely in the glob of sap, its wings
heavy as a brass angel's, until it is
all at once still, a dark speck
in a bubble of sap
oozing from the felled tree
in a forest marked for the mill.

How many millennia will pass
before a tear-drop lavaliere of amber
carrying its cargo of loss
will adorn the vanity of another
creature, the fly a fossil of a species
no longer present on the Earth,
the Earth itself a speck in a cosmos where
galaxies are carded like cotton on a comb
and pulled out into a distance
where some new fabric is being spun
and shimmers in the firelight
of countless burning suns.

IN THAT DAWN

"Bliss was it in that dawn to be alive,
But to be young was very Heaven!"
—Wordsworth

We thought if we brought the statue down, the bronze
        man on a horse, the tyrant-hero, if we held the old
                armor up to the light, till it faded to a ghostly
scrim, then the sun would pour through, the doors
        swing open, the window shades fly up of their own accord,
                and all would be well in the public square, the buckets
lifted from the central fountain would overflow
        with a clear water, the man on the cross would step down,
                put on his clothes, and—a feather in his jaunty hat
and a walking stick for the mountains—wave goodbye,
        taking with him and away forever the bleeding ikon
                of tortured flesh as an object of veneration. And the bells,
the bells would play Mozart in the towers, and a fresh breeze
        would set the wind chimes playing, and—of course—
                birds, not seen in decades, would nest again
in the blossoming branches—oh, it was a good
        dream, really, though now it lies in a child's book,
                and the library in which the book stood, on a low
shelf that a child could reach, is burned to the ground,
        and the child with it; the city is under curfew, helmeted men
                patrol the ruined streets, where nothing stands but

the bunkers—not the statues of the old founders,
    not the wall made entirely of mosaic tiles, not
        the firehouse with its great carved doors, nor the sandwich
shop on the corner where, on his blanket, the little
    terrier slept, nose in his paws, and his dreams sweet.

AFTER THE TSUNAMI

No point anymore in thinking
about the big wave, a thought
you once could ride to oblivion,
a way out of a bad story, end time,
the way the Peter Weir film pulled out
the stops like hairpins, let down
its big surprise—horizon gone, the sky
falling . . .
                white-out, the Last Wave
that ended the film, solved everything
in one final dissolve to a blank screen.

And it was all gone: conquest's white
uneasy cast, the aboriginals who saw,
drawing with sticks in the sand,
how it would come, night vision
enviable to the ones who invented light
they could switch off, hold oceans
on a strip of film, a trick of the lens,
director's cut: the sea pulls out, and out,
earth shifting its plates
as if a giant turned in his sleep—
and it all comes roaring back,
oblivion's wet wall, ground zero in motion . . .
but it wasn't like Weir's white-out,

only the credits coming up—
it wasn't like that at all.

———

Imagine those believers
who think "the Rapture" is for them,
who think of themselves virtually
lifted above the multitudes,
distanced from it all on the big screen
in the blue sky of a cruel delusion—
while below, the stinking beaches are littered
with bodies, and searching among them,
the desolate, like women gleaning the fields
after the harvest is done.

As if Noah, when the waters of the flood drew back,
when he saw what the waves had wrought,
could have exulted. Or the dove, with its green
meaning, returned to his trembling hand.

WHAT IT HINGES ON

When everything is going
just one way, and seems to be
headed for a cul-de-sac
or some stunning culmination . . .

all at once, a creak (as a rusty hinge
warns of an intruder in the night) —
the wind from another quarter
takes the sail, the cage door opens
or the lid slams shut: and all our
plans are so much smoke, a handful
of torn paper, confetti in the air
that swirls—a letter here, a sentence
there, years of work litter the field
that lies outside the town that flood
or fire took back, as the great tectonic
plates grind out their harmonics
below the sea, and the earth turns
in its restless sleep, spun
by what we cannot see, the hand
that is no hand, but brings us calm
to think it so, and think it ours
to smite our enemies,
forgetting
as we turn it to a fist,
it is ourselves curled, blind
as newborn kittens, in the palm.

THINKING ABOUT UNAMUNO'S *SAN MANUEL BUENO, MÁRTIR*

San Manuel   the priest who kept
his poor parish in the faith
burnished their bright hope of heaven
(*hope is the thing with feathers*)

it is best not to think these days
about what   what the newspapers report so reasonably
  (*I lived in the first century of world wars,
  most mornings I would be more or less insane*)
today's weather   an endless rain of feathers

when the passenger pigeon   now extinct
had not yet been converted
to fashion   slaughtered   its plumage plucked
for the elegant hats of America's women
  (*those catlike immaculate creatures
                for whom the world works*)
when the migrating flocks still passed
overhead   a billion strong   the farmers said
bird lime turned the woods white
the sky was dark for a week

And San Manuel? Late in the story we learn
he did not believe in the hope
he kept alive   believing as he did
(like his author) in the sustaining power
of fiction.

SITE VISIT

By then doctors and poets
Would have found a cure for prayer
—Fady Joudah

A cure for prayer, and the long vigil at the gates,
nostalgia's broken bubbles in the blood, aneurysm
of a dream; the double helix like a winding

stair, a twisted vine on which the monkeys climb,
(*the way up is the way down*); they live on captive
air in the cages we construct—please think

of bleak confinement, steel walls; think of Virgil
by the sinkhole at the mouth of Hell, beckoning;
he points: above on His throne of clouds

sits Majesty in burnished robes, below
the fires roast the burning flesh of those
who must be guilty of what was done

to them, agonies it took genius to describe—
didn't we understand that the punishment fits
the crime?—though the damned were from a distant

time: we had to search the footnotes for their names.
Hell is the dungeon where God's shadow falls,
cast by the monumental, obdurate cliff

that sits beside a restless sea, whose migrant waves
keep eating at its face, pulling it slowly down,
turning the intractable to sand, grain by grain,

motes in the burning eye of sun, while
fish hawks prey along the changing shore;
what breaks upon the broken rocks is spray.

BACK THEN, WE CALLED IT "THE WAR"

And though, since that time, I have read many books,
have followed the smoke trail of countless thoughts
rising from the burning libraries;
though I have inquired in the ruins of many cities,
in the writing on the fallen walls,
in the blank stares of skulls in the killing fields,
in places hidden and open:
nevertheless, I do not understand.

For though, when as a child, I watched the news unreel
at the movies: the smoke and guns, the stirring symphonic music
rousing the blood, the black-and-white legions marching
on film, the flare of anti-aircraft guns, the little planes turning
in a slow spiral as they went down in flames, the heavy-bellied
bombers opening their doors, and the bombs falling,
and where each one fell, a rising pillar of fire; and though
the voice of the announcer was manly and confident, the news
always good, we were winning, we were certainly winning, and
everyone was so proud, and collected cans, and went without
nylons and chewing gum and butter, and clustered around radios
speaking in hushed tones as if in a holy place:
nevertheless I did not understand.

And though, since that time, I have followed Freud's trail, and Adler's,
tracked bad parents, bacteria, the rotting culture in the Petri dish,
followed Nietzsche to the knife in Raskolnikov's hand, with Pip
have seen God's foot on the treadle of the loom, watched goats lick
the pillar of salt that is the whole history of grief; though
I have followed Socrates into the bathhouses of Athens, observed
how he drank the poison that certainty decrees to doubt;
though I have watched 10,000 Iagos ply betrayal's artful
trade; though I have looked in my own heart,
and knowing myself no better than most, and worse than many,
nevertheless, I do not understand.

For, today, when I follow the signs of distress
back to their source, I find only mourners
weeping at the cemetery we have made
of what was once their home.
And playing in the rubble, a little girl
who will never understand, who
nevertheless
is picking up stone after stone,
trying to piece it together again.

THE SHOW MUST GO ON

I just want to remember
the dead piled high behind the curtain.
—Mahmoud Darwish

The play had been staged as long as we could remember,
a sordid drama in which truth kept changing sides,
the name of the enemy was never the same;

sometimes the players poured over the edge
of the proscenium, spilling into the audience,
who ran terrified from the house

that had become a scene of massacre; sometimes
the drama played at a distance relaxingly remote,
caught and burnished in the bright little

dollhouse screen, so far away it was no more
than fireflies in a bottle, mere hiccups of light—
the carpet bombing, the village, torched.

So that—unless the street were yours,
and the terrible crying of the wounded
your own—it was impossible

to tell what was real, so much was not
what it seemed, was simply *not*:
not at all, not anymore, not this, not that—

yet the music was upbeat, the messenger
smiling, the voiceover a reassuring pour
of syrup in the artificial light. Meanwhile,

though the labels changed, and the set
was rearranged for every act—the plot
remained unvarying, never veering off

from the foretold end. So, when the curtain falls,
we know for certain what is going to be
piled high behind it. Yet we wait, we go on

waiting, as if the bodies might still move,
the actors untwine themselves from the pile,
step through the opening in the folded-back curtain

into the brightly lit house, the resounding applause,
the audience pulling on coats to go home,
the silent streets filling again with laughter and talk;

while deep within the darkened hall, the actors
by their lit mirrors, lift from their sweat-soaked
faces, the eyeless masks.

MAGNIFICAT

When he had suckled there, he began
to grow: first, he was an infant in her arms,
but soon, drinking and drinking at the sweet
milk she could not keep from filling her,
from pouring into his ravenous mouth,
and filling again, miraculous pitcher, mercy
feeding its own extinction . . . soon he was
huge, towering above her, the landscape,
his shadow stealing the color from the fields,
even the flowers going gray. And they came
like ants, one behind the next, to worship
him—huge as he was, and hungry; it was
his hunger they admired most of all.
So they brought him slaughtered beasts:
goats, oxen, bulls, and finally, their own
kin whose hunger was a kind of shame
to them, a shrinkage; even as his was
beautiful to them, magnified, magnificent.

The day came when they had nothing left
to offer him, having denuded themselves
of all in order to enlarge him, in whose
shadow they dreamed of light: and that
is when the thought began to move, small
at first, a whisper, then a buzz, and finally,

it broke out into words, so loud they thought
it must be prophecy: they would kill him,
and all they had lost in his name would return,
renewed and fresh with the dew of morning.
Hope fed their rage, sharpened their weapons.

And who is she, hooded figure, mourner now
at the fate of what she fed? And the slow rain,
which never ends, who is the father of that?
And who are we who speak, as if the world
were our diorama—its little figures moved
by hidden gears, precious in miniature, tin soldiers,
spears the size of pins, perfect replicas, history
under glass, dusty, old fashioned, a curiosity
that no one any longer wants to see,
excited as they are by the new giant, who feeds
on air, grows daily on radio waves, in cyberspace,
who sows darkness like a desert storm,
who blows like a wind through the Boardrooms,
who touches the hills, and they smoke.

Two

"Mission Accomplished" — The Bush/Cheney Years

ESTABLISHMENT

Death had established himself in the Red Room,
the White House having become his natural
abode: chalk-white facade, pillars like the bones
of extinct empires, armed men crawling its halls
or looking down, with suspicion, from its roof;
its immense luxury, thick carpets, its plush velvet chairs—
all this made Death comfortable, bony as he is, a fact
you'd barely notice, his camouflage a veil of flesh
drawn over him, his tailor so adroit, and he so elegant,
so GQ, almost a dandy, so suited for the tables
where the crystal, silverware, the swans of ice gleamed
with the polished purity of light on precious things;
Death was the guest of honor here, confiding, convivial
among friends who leaned to light his cigar—his power
seemed their own, body counts at their command;
a power beyond even their boy-wet dreams
was now a custom they feared to lose: each saw
the world the way a hooded falcon on the fist
sees it, blind, waiting for the next release; one word
could bury villages alive, could send
battalions to an early grave—

                                        so Death can rest
assured, smiling at such a harvest—and so
deliciously unseasonable, like berries in winter.
Welcome houseguest, he stretches his ancient

frame, warm under expensive wool, sipping wine,
picking his teeth with a last bone,
meat all the sweeter for being
the lambs of honor, corn-fed and unsuspecting;
or the children playing in the rubble
who reach down for a souvenir of steel
that has fallen from the sky—really,
Death has seldom had a better season or such
a winning score; he must see to their protection,
these little men who think to be *his* master—
flatter a fool and make him useful, he thinks,
and smiles, benignly, whitely, at his hosts,
assuring them of his gratitude, his presence
at their councils, his everlasting support . . .
until, no longer able to hide
his triumph, his delight, forgetting the flesh
he has clothed himself in for the occasion,
he rubs his hands together
in the ancient gesture of satisfaction,
naked bone on bone—how the sound grates,
how the grateful sparks fly!

WINTER LAMBS

. . . He's sad,
but sadder for his scene; the God
who made it only made it once.
—Maurice Manning

They say that winter lambs are bad, knock-kneed, greedy
for the milk of ewes who aren't their own, wheedlers,
quarrelsome, not at all what lambs are meant
to be: all fleece and friendliness; in iconography,
a glass enhancement to the gentle Shepherd
in the sunlit window of an English country church—a sign
we've learned to read. But now the fields are white
with winter lambs, their bleating thin, querulous
and full of blame, they sneer at last spring's lambs,
tear up the grass of other flocks, whatever they want, they take,
arrogant with envy like the bastard spawn of errant
rams, born on the wrong side of the field, out of season—

he's sad, but sadder for his scene, the once and future kingdom
of the lamb, where season followed season in the customary way,
where spring meant lambs, and fall a filling in of fleece,
the faithful dog to bring the herd back home—it was no
ideal world, but as it was you could expect a certain

alternation of day and night, spring and fall, and not
unbroken dark, this freezing winter without end,
hope foreclosed while being born, those young
who've never known a warming air, the shade
of leafy summer trees, the scent of lilac by the fence—
those once recurrent things that now seem made but once.

RENDITION, WITH FLAG

The net was spread last night, catching beavers
who have been teething on the trees.

Around the bend, the verge is littered
with gnawed trees, some scraped raw
at the base, some fallen, some about to fall.
The lights of the hunters star the pond.

Thanksgiving? It is a time of anguish,
secrets bagged and hidden under silken flags,
stripes stretched to breaking at the threads,
stars darkening from an unseen source,
red seeping out of all the straining seams.
A US soldier smokes, while Fallujah burns.

The cold is growing now, ice waits in the wings.
The beavers all removed, or fugitive,
dead leaves begin to settle in the silt,
the work of winter will go on, dislodging
what the earnest animals had built.

Thanksgiving 2004

POSTCARD WITH STATUE OF LIBERTY, NO MESSAGE

Impassive? Yes. Standing stone, crown of brass,
drapes of granite, tits of steel. Impervious. Impasse.
When the woman with the torch has had her lights
shot out, snipers from the factory of lies, gnats
from the sodden swamps of shredded files, rats
biting and biting, and everyone pretending not
to notice the rising welts, the caught breath,
the throes, the imperatives of venom, wealth.

They said it couldn't happen here. It happened
anyway, while the freedom fries sizzled, the gas
flames keeping the oil in a frenzy of heat
until you felt nothing: the myelin sheath, the fat
wrapping every nerve melted down—exposed,
the nerves: power lines brought down, torn hoses
spouting fire—gaping mouth, ignited breath.
Sun sunk in the west, she—backlit in the river Lethe.

COLD DAWN OF THE DAY WHEN BUSH WAS
ELECTED FOR A SECOND TERM

I am jealous today   of my dog   of his ignorance of all this
of his unerring instinct   for what matters   and his general aesthetic
    for meat   and his inability to vote
against his own best interests   and while I am ruing
    the cold   the skimpy souls   the blizzard of ignorance
(the big price   so many keep paying for that)   I think
    of the old man   from the Inupiat village   of Barrow
a place that sits on the edge   of the frozen Arctic ocean
    and burns   in the midnight sun of summer   where
the snowcats have replaced   the old dog sleds   sleek
    metal noses pointing   toward the place where   snow
when it returns   comes from   and the old man says to me
    the snowcats are fine all right   but you know
he says   his mind filling   with the blizzards   of ninety winters
    if there's a whiteout   the dogs'll get you home

THE RAVEN'S TEXT

The raven did not return. For everywhere she flew
was barren, the trees gone, dead hands
still reaching through the mud
of aftermath—the waters had left nothing
but a desecration. She flew the whole, huge curve
of Earth, seeing, as she went, the turning heavens
and the way the sun rose as she flew into night,
a growing sun so strong it lit the sodden world
in stark detail, unbearable—so she flew higher,
far and farther still, till she was dizzy with altitude,
a tiny, black and winged trace in that bright
sky, a mote in the cold blue eye of heaven;
turned in her circling, cawing flight, dark
into dark, far beyond the docile dove
on its errand of conventional return,
carrying its requisite bit of green to celebrate
the survival of the chosen
few: the many lost (their bloated, discarded
carcasses) kept carefully from scripture, and from view.

THE METEOR

was falling, and nothing could stop it.
The day was bright, but the shadow growing.
(*Like the shadow of a great rock in a weary land,*
Thou art . . .) The whole history of human hope
a shambles, wrecked toys in a rubble of stone,
a cracked chalice, spilled wine, blood's
masquerade undone. Overhead, the meteor,
growing. What use a childish faith,
hosannas, *Our Father*s; what use
the cradle of stars, that, in precession, slip
slowly into new constellations
as galaxies spiral and spin, eating back
their stray matter?
                    Standing
on a promontory, Earth, our little hatchery,
among the other forms of life, mute—
we too grow speechless before the burgeoning
shadow. While the mind arriving
at the end of its thoughts, their usefulness,
paces lonely in its cage of bone, like the sibyl
cursed to live on, century after century,
as the meteor approached, and she,
in grief, foreknowing its arrival
(*Rock of Ages, comfort me . . .*)
through so many years of false belief

filling the mass graves—as if death
could be mastered by serving it.

The slowly descending mass,
the long-awaited heaven lowering
itself (*on earth as it is in heaven*)—

the bloody altar stone our species has made
of its own habitation, set now, like a gemstone,
a solid darkness against the wheeling sky,
its fall toward Earth imperceptible, except
for the growing dark in which we live.

HIGH NOON

The soul is not so clean & white
as Kleenex; as old Faust dramatized,
it can be sold for a dram of power,

it wars within, and good
struggles with not-so-good, or *vice
versa*, the soul's creatures unsure

about what's natural in selection: symbiosis
vs. dog eat dog. Uncertain about who is fit
for what, the soul scratches its itchy

ineffability, sits down on its missing rump
and thumps the somatic walls of its cage;
unable to shout, it calls (nevertheless)

on the gods of all tortured souls to buy
a ticket to the last frontier,
where souls are one thing or another,

where the borders are guarded by walls,
and the sun is forever at noon, no shadows
intrude, & two men are forever about

to reach for their holsters and draw.
While God, directly above, ponders
which side to be on.

SATURDAY NIGHT

Moonlit rocks, sand, and a web of shadows
      thrown over the world from the cottonwoods,
          the manzanita, the ocotillo; it is
the hour of the tarantula, a rising
      as predictable as tide, irritable as
          moon drag. And if this were
an SF film, the spider would be
      huge as a water tank, it would loom
          red-eyed and horrible, its mandibles
wet with drool or blood, and screams
      would be heard as it stumbled
          through the cactus and the brush,
trees upended, small bodies
      crunching in its path; in the distance,
          police cars, lights flashing, sirens blaring,
would be tearing down the highways,
      dust rising in their wake, and cars
          would begin streaming from distant
cities, the terror growing with each
      report of it—the creature, like a figure
          from the bad conscience of the race,
hungry, hairy, would be coming
      for every blonde, she, hiding in a million
          bedrooms, breasts heaving under
filmy white lace . . . but now as the film
      runs down, in a rush of stale air
          the hydraulic spider deflates, the saline

leaks from the implants of the bed-
      room blonde, the moon's projection
           clicks off, and the night is as it was,
a place where fear takes its many
      forms, and the warships gather in
           a distant gulf, where a small man
with more arms than a Hindu god,
      has set a desert alight, and grief blooms;
           while here, the theaters are full
of horror on the screen, and you can hear—
           over the sinister canned music,
                the chainsaws, and the screams—
the sound of Coke sucked up through straws,
           your own jaws moving as you chew.

Three

"then all but failed to find his own
way out again . . ."

—Ovid, *Metamorphoses*, Book 8

Voices from the Labyrinth

MINOS

lean close   I am only   the echo of a voice
husk of power   king   of cobwebs   cast off shell of the cicada
the singing insect   long since flown   memory   a spectral   thread
broken   line   across the centuries   perforations
a place to tear   open again the rift in time   string of   tears

the clew   that led from one room of the dream   to the next
became   a flame   burning along a fuse   until
it lit the black night   of the Aegean
gone   our port of pleasure   there   pause again at the word
pleasure
the way wind lingers in bright air

turns hot   Sirocco stirs the nerves again   blows the dry earth
Ariadne   in a dress of dust   grows indistinct
(no, stay a moment . . .   I want to know . . .)
the dolphin leaps   only in the peeling blue   of the painted wall
a lizard brushes my foot   Theseus   only a name
for the passage of power   from one place to another

we were lovers of peace   of art   the winding measures of dance
of poems   yes   we were liars   always   new gods
thirsty for blood   swallow the old   I am tired
where are   the vineyards   the arbors
they say   the way in   is the way out   we end
at the place   of beginning   black sails   for the old kings
white   in the hold   for the next

ARIADNE

They say
I placed the clew
in his hand   (even my father   shamed   came to believe it)
but it was their story   told long after   what happened
left us beggars in our once   rich   island
before the earth erupted   before the sea rose
we were a city without walls   our complications
were within   artists   traders   worshippers
of the changing moon
we were ourselves the labyrinth
and the clew   I was she   who served the Lady
who wears the crescent   holds   the twin serpents
who is the reel
around which the thread   is wound
now   even the olive trees   nothing but   pillars of smoke
and I   standing among ruins
looked up into the eyes of Greece
fierce   bearers of spears   gods of sun   and thunder
carrying shields   on which
we were history   merely
an old dream of peace
the white bull
grazing in the wild grass
the cows deep
in perpetual
summer

the ibex   abroad in the mountain
in the field   poppies   aflame like red silks
gone   in the fiery night
the past   only a painting   crumbling from the walls
and I   a figment now
a shade   who flits
along the labyrinth   of time
history twisted like a skein of yarn
back on the spindle
back to the spinner's hand
I run my hand along   but where is the wall
where is the world
(what have they done to my brother)
of course we went mad   when they came
there was so much death
they seemed   almost its master
Daedalus   serves a new god
and I   a foreign figure
in a Greek story
the Greek key is a maze
it is *their* design   fit
for the walls of their temples of stone
finding us weak
they took what they say we gave
I shall free myself
from that fiction
as soon   as I find
the right turn
a way out
of these
lines

DAEDALUS

always there are questions   always   answers disagree
   like quarrelsome neighbors   who argue about everything
     where the fence goes   who owns the fig tree   whose god made
the world green   whose dog tore the garden up   whose story
   is true   whose story is this we are in   I should know
     I am Daedalus   artificer   artist   teller of tales   trapped
in the maze   of my own invention   Dante whirling
       in the circles of an exile's hell   vile dreams   of monsters
   the torture of my enemies   incendiary   I am   every exile
in my mind   ascending   living under   one lord after another
     I am the ringmaster   the man on the merry-go-round horse
     I am the architect   who comes home to a ruined house
Marcel   who ends one thousand pages   with a man beginning to write
   Finnegan's scribe   with the bad eyes   the many tongues
   the wake   into which we sail   to begin again
born tired   the poet   whose *way forward   is the way   back*
I   Daedalus was hired   to map the underground its twisted ways
keep it   secret   put the lid on   a painted ceiling of stars
   still   air extends itself   sun dazzles the sea
     a scatter of floating feathers   marks   the limits of art
Knossos   drowns in sand again
         gnosis   down the bloody drain   of history
   and I   only a man in search of an exit   hired   to construct it

THE MINOTAUR

Do not mistake me   I am not what you think
what you think is polluted by what you were told
if man is the measure   then   man is the monster
See   I have taken the long gold clew   in my mouth
I am reeling it in   reeling it in
a man is attached
Theseus an obsolete hero   sent long ago   this time
I have pulled the knife   from the heart of the plot
even as I pull the line   that   he holds in his hand
and thinks it his own   see   I am drawing him
closer and closer   I can smell his fear now
the line he believed would lead him out is
pulling him   inexorably in   I never
let go I was born under the sign of
Taurus we hold on   whatever
we've got stays caught
I am hauling and
hauling
until
we
are
face to face
you are looking
into my eyes
I into yours
now you see who we are
tangled in

the spiraling threads
that curl
round and round
the central
axis
of the double helix
along
the nucleotides
of creation
where the past
is always
with us
and always open
to change
I have met you here
because
it is time
there is so much past
it is late
just time enough
for an exit

MEDITATION ON DNA WITH GENE SPLICES
FROM SHAKESPEARE'S SONNETS

The argument all bare

The caduceus leaned against the wall beside
the door, forgotten there, as if it had been left
by chance, then overlooked, and stayed.
Its axis—tall rolled cardboard—was a painted gold,
thin gilt through which gray fibers showed,
and curled around it, in a double weave, two
snakes, one blue, the other red, papier-mâché,
covered with a high sheen paint, so when
it caught the swaying light, they seemed to writhe.

It had stood in the corner of the costume room
as long as the dresser could remember,
and was to him a kind of relic, something
of which he had almost a holy fear, so
hadn't dared to throw it out, or even move it
from its place beside the door. And over time,
like all those things forever there, it had become
invisible, something you stopped attending to,
which disappeared—until the day that it was gone.

vanishing, or vanished out of sight

The gods are wise to us, and must have known we'd miss
the clue, the key to immortality hidden in plain view.
At first their messenger had carried it; you could
see him lounging at the mouth of hell, or leaning
on a sign at the crossroads, pointing two ways
at once; the serpents kept him company, as
did his shadow when the day was fine. But like the air
from a leaking tire, belief went out of him—he became
mere far-fetched fiction from another time.

The crow, or dove, it shapes them

In the unseen generative within, the double helix
writhes, writing the past into its present forms,
and sends invention down the howling chutes
of time. Do the serpents on the staff grow mutinous,
restless under scrutiny? They twist and twist,
their hissing is a steady sound, as if a fury
built within, life at its center squirms—
the crow walks, raucous, on the lawn,
the dove does what doves do: it coos and coos.

And delves the parallels

in this but shadow play, the great stone amphi-
theaters rubble now, the tragic players long since gone
to television, risen gods, and falling bombs.
Image has been swallowed by its once-secret source

(the chick returns to the egg), a crystal ball that tells
who bedded who back when, what broken coupling
haunts the family line, what harm, inborn, will end it all.
Excuse not silence so? What more is there to say?
What secret left to keep? Hermes laughs, picks up
his staff, and, whistling, walks away.

AN ODE TO ASYMMETRY

Perfectibility, unearthly thing, abstract,
what clings to it is neither root nor soil
nor any *thing*, but evanescent, scentless
thought, a hovercraft that crosses on twin foils,
back and forth the agitated waters of the mind,
and never lands. And what it crosses, it negates;
it crosses out.
             Like the anti-matter
of the universe, with all of matter's properties
reversed: when it meets a particle of
matter, the pair annihilate each other—
in their place: pure energy, radiant light,
as if destruction were divine. Not so!
For symmetry is broken from the start,
from which all things descend, and here we are.

When the universe began—Creation
as Big Bang—for reasons science can
not explain, the balance tipped toward
matter: more was made of matter
than of its absent anti-matter twin.
Perfect symmetry would have meant
pure annihilation, that nothingness
of which both Indian saint
and French logician

dream, exquisite binary machine—
Being and Nothingness: *ka-boom*.

And knowing that, the thought, ideal,
which these lines at first unearthed, dissolves,
a cloud that had obscured the sun:
the ocean waves continue as before, embrace
with foam the swimmer on her board
(each bubble a lens to catch the light),
the mountain rises from the ocean's floor,
and out in space, the galaxies spin on,
the stars wink back at everything:
root, plant, orangutan,
blue planet, rutabaga, kitchen sink.

TO THINK WHAT WE MIGHT HAVE . . .

Today—Pompeii,
on view: the ultimate interruption,
permission to blame nature for the failure
to finish anything—to bake the bread, to put
the kids to bed on time, sew the tattered toga, ice
the wine, draw up your will, take the swill out back
to feed the pigs, do some small kindness to the poor,
write your senator (you hear that Rome's gone
rotten, and your taxes will be used for yet
another war) . . .

            but never mind, when the smoke
and ash rain down, the mountain extending
its huge domain, the lava pouring in through
every door, night visiting by day—a final, solid
fact, the darkness closing down on the Poet's
House, her dog, and *cave canem* in mosaic tile
on the floor; that poem will not be written
she had planned, the one whose lines, so elegant,
when scanned, would make the mighty Virgil
weep with shame; the poem of 1,000 lines
that would be sung for 1,000 years—begun
just then, word one, it promised to make
effusive springs break forth from stone,
and warlike hearts repent their hardened ways,
and poor nostalgic Orpheus lay down his lyre

for good (and keep his head): this would have
come to pass—but for Vesuvius, a jealous
nature pouring its hot wrath on all her drafts,
while filling up the beds, the future,
with its furious furnace breath—ah, such
a memorable excuse, catastrophic death—

                                        but hey,
the tour is tiresome, the day is cold; in town
there are a dozen shops displaying skeletons
of bats, the Tears of Christ, and Davids, Davids
by the gross, effigies for sale at any price.

FOUR FLATS, GETTING DARK SOON, NOTHING TO DO BUT WALK

for Bob Zieff's "Sad Walk"

Walk it: the long hall of the horn,
passage of amber, trumpet of honey,
sweet, unbearably sad. Walk it: the bridge over
troubled waters, deep complaint of the bass, wind
making the guy wires hum. Walk it: piano,
bucket of jewels swinging
on the shoulder of a girl from a far
province, the percussion of stones
and the high stretch of her voice, singing,
as the stones play against the bright metal
of the bucket's rim. Walk the path
that winds between notes, step
between dark hedges of sound, the green
notes depending on the aisles of silence,
the soul pushing its cart up the empty rows,
arms drawing the bow across strings,
the slide of the horn, back and forth,
the shuttle drawn in, pulling the string
through, drawing it out—as the leaves turn
restless and rustling on the branch, sheets
billow out on the line, the grasses bend—the night
is coming on, the air cooling fast:
below, a man, drawing his collar
closed and his coat tighter around him, stopping

there, under a streetlight, for a moment,
gathering the light around him like a shawl,

he lifts his trumpet to the moth-swarm of the stars,
pauses, an interval like a held breath, then
he is walking it, walking out on it
across a bottomless canyon of air, nothing
but the song to sustain him, walking
those long notes home.

LIKE I REALLY LIKE THAT

Beverley said, though you could barely hear her
from where we sat, high on the slopes
of the local mountain, the snow beginning
to give way to spring, absorbing the sound
in its softening drifts. An odd place for
the premiere of a play, but Bev believed in
the mountain, knows it's in for some fancy
erosion, and fancies that—and she wants
a vista as part of the plot. Just then, Jon says:
*I don't know anything about it, but
I know what I like.* I think that's what
Beverley meant when she said *I really like
that*, because they were talking about what
a Japanese cosmetic company calls
Beautiful Human Life, which is what
Beverley's play is about—moving, as it does,
between pine trees and palmettos, cutting a wide
swath across the little planet where we bunk
and play musical instruments and torch
villages. And this is where I say: *consider
the heart* (though they are attending
to the play and pay me no mind), *the heart*,
I return to my subject, *is a treadmill
in a drawing by Escher, as it moves
up and down, in and out, taking us*

with it—the rooms change, but it is
uncertain whether you are going
on, or returning where you once
began—a problem of perspective and
memory. But now Beverley's play is moving
toward its denouement; the chorus is
singing like mad, wearing costumes made
of rabbit hair and silk, they are praising
the great goat of spring, so loud
their praise, and with so much heat,
that the snow beneath us begins to move,
and we are sliding (no way to slow this down)
at ever accelerating speeds, along with the tons
of snow, it's all going now, and we're riding it,
all's a blur, the trees a green fur, a fuzz,
the wind a cold blast in your face—
but that Beverley! She knows a bad ending
when she sees it—and she calls it off:
to hell with the trope, the slope, the whole
blessed thing: she is almost shouting now,
and hitting her tambourine, and the badgers
and marmots that line the path, holding
their glowing lanterns against the night,
have picked up the beat, and one by one,
as we all sing the chorus, they swing
their little lights, and the whole hill rocks.

ENCOUNTER IN THE LOCAL PUB

Unlike Francis Bacon, we no longer believe
in the little patterns we make of the chaos of history.
—overheard remark

As he looked up from his glass, its quickly melting ice,
into the bisected glowing demonic eyes of the goat,
he sensed that something fundamental had shifted,

or was done. As if, after a life of enchantment, he
had awakened, like Bottom, wearing the ears of an ass,
and the only light was a lanthorn, an ersatz moon.

It was not that the calendar hadn't numbered the days
with an orbital accuracy, its calculations
exact, but like a man who wants to hang a hammock

in his yard, to let its bright net cradle him, but only
has one tree, so he—wild and aware of it—knew
he had lost the order he required, and with it, rest—

his thoughts only a sagging bundle of loose ends,
and the heart, a naked animal in search of a pelt,
that once fell for every Large Meaning it could

wrap itself in, as organs are packed in ice for transit
from one ending to the next, an afterlife of parts—and
the whole? Exorbitant claim—not less than all,

and oddly spelled; its ear rhyme is its opposite,
the great hole in the heart of things. The goat,
he noticed, had a rank smell, feral. Unnerved,

he looks away, watches the last of his ice
as it melts, the way some godlike eye might see
the mighty glaciers in a slow dissolve back into sea.

He notes how incommensurate the simile, a last
attempt to dignify his shaking gaze, and reaches
for the bill; he's damned if the goat will pay.

Four

"I was left behind with the
immensity of existing things."

—Czesław Miłosz

WHAT LOVES, TAKES AWAY

If the nose of the pig in the market of Firenze
has lost its matte patina, and shines, brassy,
even in the half light; if the mosaic saint
on the tiles of the Basilica floor is half gone,
worn by the gravity of solid soles, the passing
of piety; if the arms of Venus have reentered
the rubble, taken by time, her perennial lover,
mutilating even the memory of beauty;
                                        and if
the mother, hiding with her child from
the death squads closing in,
if she, trying to keep the child
quiet, to keep them from being found out,
holds her hand over his mouth, holds him
against her, tighter and tighter, until he stops
breathing;
            if the restorer—trying to bring back
to perfection the masterpiece scarred by its
transit through time, wipes away
by mistake, the mysterious smile . . .
                                    if what
loves, and love is, takes away what it aims
to preserve,
            then here is the place to fall
silent, meaning well but in danger
of marring what we would praise, unable

to do more than wear down the marble
steps to the altar, smother the fire
we would keep from the wind's extinction,

                                       or if, afraid
of our fear, we lift the lid from the embers, and send
abroad, into the parched night, a flight of sparks,
incendiary, dying to catch somewhere,
hungry for fuel, the past, its dry provision
tinder for brilliance and heat, prelude
to cold, and to ash . . .

RESTORED TO BLUE

and the famous cloud
she wiped away
with the wrong solvent . . .

Inadvertence, when the mind, distracted by sun
playing in the leaves, slips, destroys the work.
As if the work were meant to stay, the days
not on a string that each night cuts, and only
memory, which fades, and other bits of matter
carrying order in their cells (give or take a broken
chain or two, a mutant moment in a copy-cat
world)—only these remain. While what we are,
the lived-in days, the irreplaceables we love,
these—like the famous cloud, though painted
by a master's hand (long gone)—are wiped away
by solvent time, an endless surf, a changing shore.

So much for restoration's care, the delicate brush,
restraint in the retouching, all the shoring up,
the dutifully kept files that one day soon will fill
recycle bins—such things are everyday and are
not news. So look away, or look: today the sky
is cloudless as a canvas used exclusively for blue,

and filling in the blanks seems nothing more
than sport, a game to leave behind, a way to keep
the mind from knowing that the blanks, though
time and time filled in, return: a cloudless sky
we're meant to read as happiness, and so we do.

VERMEER'S GIRL, A RESTORATION

An erotic intensity that demands something just as real and human in return. The
relationship may be only with an image, yet it involves all that art is supposed to
keep at bay. —Edward A. Snow, *A Study of Vermeer*, 1979

For an instant, I see her, before her face was cliché,
where she hung, on the wall by the front door,
at the foot of the staircase, in the little house
of our childhood, and floated above us, a presence,
always there, silent, by the Dutch-style
door, whose top we swung open in summer.

They have sullied *The Girl with the Pearl Earring*,
subjected her to their prurient gaze — novelized,
eroticized, reduced her to gossip and innuendo,
backstoried her as servant, thorn in the side
of a wife, object of desire, poverty's child, mute
with class diffidence and awe, as if she could be
aware of posterity's view of the painter—all this
from a mysterious glow and unreadable expression,
the illusion of being seen by her gaze, a shimmer
of pearl, brush strokes of lapis lazuli, crushed
to intensify blue.
                    Overexposed, even in film,
where they followed her to her family's dark
hovel, to the wet stones of the market where

she met the butcher's son she would marry
for meat—my god, couldn't they leave her
alone, in the nether region of art where she is,
so beautifully, no one—not servant, or mistress,
or his daughter Maria, but anonymous,
secret, what no one can name, pure mystery
of being, restored across time
by art, which keeps nothing at bay.

TREES, EVEN AT THIS DISTANCE

have not quite lost their dreamlike sheen,
a glimmer that quietly outshines the living wood,
emanations from the forests of the mind—

in the half-recall, awake and walking
the fall streets—the sudden memory
of those trunks: so tall, the highest branches
were lost in the blinding light; the bark
of each one seamed and split, as if the tree
had opened, all along its length, an invitation
to the hungers of the air,
                              for astride each
trunk, woodpeckers walked its wall,
racheting up and down—
                              but, inexplicably,
the woods which should be resonant
with the percussive sound of hunting beaks,
were still, a silence penetrating
as those beaks, but different in kind,
benign, as if the scene were charmed:
no predation, and not the slightest hint of harm.

The birds were beautiful in the flicker
way: black and white, strobed as they moved
in the filtered light that pours through
groves of trees—with now and then

a splash of red along the throat or
on the flicker's head. I watched and
waited for the scene to make itself
more clear, something that might be named,
something for the waking self
to take away—some sign: a feather
left on the bedroom floor, a smear of
tree sap on the cheek, mud clinging to
the soles of shoes . . .

                    What lingers needs
no talisman: the silver, fissured trunks,
the moving birds going up and down—
the dream a Jacob's ladder.

THE PALEST FLOWERS / ASH, SNOW . . .
Constance Merritt, "Partial Rose"

Winter in the words, flakes of snow
the only flowers, abundance of
perfected cold that keeps the ground
so warm. Buried there, no
grave, but the hibernating bear,
huge in his den, slowly using summer's
feast in the silent night of winter,
pulse idling, brain grown
somnolent, his life the slow hum
of the system turned down low,
fuel efficient, sweet sleep,
though, now and then, a light
glimmers on the drowsing
river of a dream, where
the bright salmon forever swim
upstream . . .
                    the great fur
mound of the bear stirs
as the fish leaps, the paw's out
in a flash of claws, closes
on the flailing muscle;
in dream, it is all good: the leap,
the catch, the helpless clash
of appetites—one for the home
stream, one for flesh against winter—

while outside, the snow softly falls
thicker and thicker, holding
the creature who sleeps
curled like a hand
in the warm mitten
of earth, unaware of
the cold world above:
backs bending, curses,
the scraping of shovels—
that softness,
its terrible weight.

LARGER TO THOSE WHO STAY

After the blight, the year
when the pines had succumbed
and the once-green air grew gray
with sawdust from the teeth
of steel that gnawed the dead trees
down—that year the exodus
began. For weeks departure
clogged the roads; they left in droves,
unable to bear for long the bareness
and the lack of shade—the way the sun
beat down on the iron griddle
of the ground; the way the wind,
without the pines to play, had grown
silent, moving across the empty
land, like a hand on an unstrung harp.

But for those of us who stayed, the absence
of the trees grew larger, and with it,
the sky, which began its vast retreat
into the past, light years away. Like the dark
matter of the universe that can't be seen
or known except by its effects,
the absence of the pines
changed the shape of things,
and like the distant stars, the galaxies,
whose speed defies the laws of gravity,

and inexplicably increases as they disappear
from view, the empty groves began to grow
from some dark energy, defying even
the laws of friction in the local air:
the swing you stop pushing slows down.

We walk in the mind's dark shades now,
in the green blur of the missing pines,
and the wind plays again in the lost
branches, where the fallen nests hang,
and the unborn birds—my god, how they sang.

WELCOME TO THE DOLLAR BIN

      its glints of glass, flattering
tricks of light—as a disco ball
      of mirrors, turning on a wire
in the overheated currents of the air,
      tosses off a dazzling shower of dots,
the way a dog coming out of a lake
      shakes a flurry of sparkling drops—
the dollar bin overflows with
      has beens, loose sequins, plastic
rings, pin heads without the pins,
      sequence lost, a smattering
of this and thats, tins and tins of
      peppermints, miscellaneous
mini-things, lost charms, letters from
      a Scrabble set, a scrambled
alphabet, confetti of an old intent,
      and what was pure
astonishment, a glittering dust
      begging for attention in the bin.

MEDITATION ON LINES FROM SHAKESPEARE'S SONNET 73

For Julia Randall, 1923–2005

When yellow leaves, or none, or few, do hang . . .
How precious are the few remaining leaves
when prefaced by the absence of them all.

Clear, how less makes dear, and how the iambs
fall like leaves, discrete, how commas keep
the beat, like hinges swing the sounds.

But most of all, I love this line because
I hear by heart, when that "do hang"
rings at line's end, the deeper sound,

past tense, pure lyric knell: *bare ruined choirs*
where late the sweet birds sang. And then
I think of Wordsworth (whom I do not love),

his "Lines" above the ruined abbey open
to the sky, whose monks once made those
choirs sing, the little birds of God, gone but for

the bard's sweet line—a loveliness that,
like a levee, stands against the rising
tide of real time: there, where the river bends,

and, on its banks, the town of Hay-on-Wye,
house after house, room after room of old
and musty books, even the barns piled high,

books smelling of mildew and decay, of leather
rotting in the damp. And there I found a book
I sent to you (who loved Wordsworth with

a true abandonment), uncompromising you—
a book in which some addled man had thought
to act as critic of the songs of birds: for each,

he set a little line of notes, and then, as if
he were a music critic at a concert hall,
he let us know exactly what the songs were

worth, and some he praised, but most of them
dismissed, and told, in no uncertain terms,
their flaws. So, it was to you, fierce critic

of the failed melodies of mediocrity,
winnower with your own pitch perfect ear—
I sent that little book as a kind of inside

joke you'd understand. You, who move
now in memory alone, and in those poems
of yours, *where late the sweet birds sang.*

HARMONY BOWL

We none of us knew who named it that, the hollow,
      the place where nothing would grow. Seemed like
a likely place, sheltered by hills, but a kind of mold
      had taken over, living off the rotting damp of fallen
trees and the debris of what was once alive.
      The air was thick with spores, and more than
one man had grown ill and dizzy when he tried
      to homestead there, and some had died. Word was
that in the old days, two roving players chanced by, and
      settled in the hollow when the axle on their wagon
split, and their last horse gave up the ghost. Some
      said they had run mad, and war was in the why of it,
something that they couldn't bear. They were
      a pair—his act was swallowing a sword, and hers
was juggling fire. He wore the motley of the harlequin,
      the belled hat of the Fool; she, the velvet cloak
of a player queen; they plied their dying trade
      till no one came to see it played, till it was
clear that theirs was a twice-told tale no one cared
      to hear—but it was all they had to tell, together
with tricks of the blade and how to catch the falling fire.

      When the climate changed, the little hollow, sweetly
cradled in the hills, became a sieve that soaked up
      every drop of the endless rain, and, helped by clouds
that never broke, the mold began its slow

encroachment, filament on filament, its minute cobweb
mass of branching threads—that looked to us
          like fur—digested in its spread whatever had
lain below, and waving its rootlike rhizomes
          in the breeze, laden with spores, the mold became
the hollow's floor, where nothing else could grow. We
          thought it would consume its hosts at last, die off.
But no. For when the food that mold requires
          disappears, it goes on in a simpler form, asexual,
like plaster statues of Our Lady—the mold, art's clone, year
          after year, makes as many copies of itself
as the trade, or mercy, hollow at the core, will bear.

COLONY COLLAPSE DISORDER (CCD)

. . . in the demise of honey bee health . . . the interaction between pesticides, diseases and varroa [mites] and the newly identified Israel acute paralysis virus (IAPV), are likely contributing factors.

Nothing more definite than that we awoke
the next morning (*were we dreaming?*) to
the same droning sound, as the bombers flew on,
named with an A, a B or an F, plus a number—
        as if the letters
of the sacred alphabet and the Arabic numerals
(so much more efficient for measuring the stars
and the playful motions of matter
than the clumsy Roman numerals, though those
were fine for incising on the foundations)—
        as if these signs
were like locusts that, once released from their shells,
spelled only death, the devouring of the grain . . .

really, we can't say anything more definite
just now (*we must have been dreaming*)—for an hour
we were like children again, our hearts
were *that* high—how we cheered
        as if to drown out
the keening, the raven caws, the orphaned
sound of the wind blowing over the ruined walls,

the F-16s going on making their runs,
and drones from the sickened hive . . .

when the beekeepers arrive to see to their bees
in the spring, the colonies have collapsed,
the dead bees tumble out like pieces from
an old game, the dried comb crumbles
at a touch, no milk and honey left to spill . . .
in the rutted rows of stumps, the olive grove
(*what were we thinking?*) cut down, the hum,
a wind in the ghostly trees,
grown louder now—dead bees
in the phosphorescent flowers
tossed in an open tomb.

SUCH STUFF AS DREAMS ARE MADE ON

"... man, you might say, is nature dreaming ..." —Robinson Jeffers

Impossible to shake, this dream, clear as the reflection
of morning in the tidal bay, dark water wearing
the cobalt and pink streaks of dawn, clouds floating
like ethereal lilies in the brightening day ...

this is the dream that was given from the first,
the high cliffs by the sea for vantage:
from such a promontory, all the carnage,
life against life below the dark waves, unseen;
while the glorious scene of a colorist god
fills the dreaming eye of the mind. This is the beauty
of distance: the place where the wind is fresh,
the rank odor of war is gone (even from memory),
the sea lions stretch on the rocks—the old boys
lifting their whiskered heads to roar, as if this were
only a chorus of joy, a sound that blends
with the roar of the waves, the whisper
of wind in the thin branches of pine, needles
like the porcupine's, that bristle at the first sign
of approach.
              Blue half-light below, the retraction
of the eel into the coral cave's dark, while the reef
breaks surf into a line of lace, the birds

are a flourish against the azure ground
of the sky, a brittle dreamscape blue that shatters
at a touch—sensing how it must feel to be the fish
caught in the claws of the hawk, helplessly watching
the ocean recede, to look down,
as the krill must, into the black endless night
of the whale's gut, to feel—as the deer
must—the sharp teeth, rending . . . but here,
the mind balks, nature begins to dream again
of its extravagant, merciless beauty
that blinds, and compels—sweet dreams
that only compassion dispels.

THE MORNING AFTER

. . . or so I once dreamed and wrote down,
until the dream became what I believed and what I wrote.
—Spencer Reece

Now it's 12-point type and you're on your own,
        the lovely lines of another's dream must shrink,
and what you think, however it was formed, is
        what you've got to live with on the brink, what
you believed, and wrote, and see!—how sweet it is to lean
        upon the hitching post of words, that tie us
to a world where we would otherwise be
        just bits of wafting chaff, fallen from the threshing fan,
gone to seed for what grows next—and who are we
        to disagree, be vexed at what we are, literate
specks of carry-on, winnowed for the grain. No bloom
        resides in theory, which makes carrion of flesh, while peonies
unfold in silks as intermittent as a season's show,
        and fashion follows vixens from their holes, while all our hope
(we'd hoped to trade our fear for that) is like the boat
        whose rotted hull leaks everywhere, the hands
are busy bailing round the clock, while ducks
        float by, and tails up, look underneath for fodder
in the mud, their beaks are green and tasseled
        with the weedy compost of the pond, while we,

keepers of the hypothetical beyond, sink slowly
     like a Northern sun in dusk, phenomenon purkinje,
violet synapse, the colors worth the disappearance
     of the light, perhaps, while in the local trees,
with just the usual winter's lapse, the sap
     can't help but rise, and rise again, while
the old mill turns its rusted wheel by rote
     in a stream whose passing water will not pass
the test of potability—if all goes well in Denmark,
     something's rotten here, and readiness, alas, may not
be all: our life, that sparrow's flight from dark to dark
     across the lighted mead hall, till darkness swallows all—
our sun a spark in boundless night, and the beacon
     of the lighted hall—a firefly in a well.

OF A WORD

English asks: What does it mean?
Italian asks: How does it want to be said?

I ask in the way of Italian, which gives to words desire,
how *gray matter* wants to be said. It lumbers
up from drowse, makes its way to water, fills its trunk,
then swings it, making of water a wide arc, in which
the sunlight is caught. Meanwhile, in the poetry class,
the instructor asks of the image: "What does it mean?"
and the elephant, which by now is a tonnage
that wants to get out of the range of reduction,
is making its way up the steep trail
of the mountain to where sky invades the peaks,
where it wraps itself in cloud, the kind of obscurity
that a wary elephant is willing to indulge in
when tracked back toward its lair.
                                   And up there,
on the cliffside, near where the clouds are drifting
in and out of the boulders, far above the tree line,
a large word, *elegy*, with a nine foot wing span,
wants to be said as a condor, one saved from
extinction and recently released to the wild.
It settles down on a bluff next to the gray
cloud which it understands as an elephant,
however obscure it appears. The condor,

who is a vulture of sorts, has dirty pink wrinkled
skin, and a cold eye, but is sensitive and quite
warm-hearted, and is pleased to consort with
the elephant in this safe aerie, where words
are said as they wish to be said—weighty or
winged as they please: heavy but light as
clouds are, or soaring in search of the dead.

HEADLONG FOR THAT FAIR TARGET

The traveller owns the grateful sense
Of sweetness near, he knows not whence . . .
—John Greenleaf Whittier, from "Snowbound"

You might have said our aim was bad,
        for we had spent years chasing it—that
sweetness near, the target that kept moving
        with the years, borne away on wings,
or in the open freight cars that rattled
        through the night across vast sweeps
of plain, or sealed in envelopes sent
        by courier from Vladivostok to Minsk—

we tracked it in the packs of mules
        making their slow way up the tortuous
paths of the Himalayas, or glimpsed
        on a backroad in Mississippi, then
lost around a bend—despite our expert aim,
        like a mirage, it always moved
before us, always just beyond, no one
        knew quite where it might be found—

and so we traveled on, read almanacs,
        picked up lingua francas, practiced our aim,
visited psychics, mystics; racked our brains,
        riffled through racks and racks of

clothes, of magazines, guide books, schedules
        for the island ferries, encyclopedias;
pursued it through the chartless ways, the Metro
        of D.C., and the sewers of *Paris*, among
the living and the dead; it led us to frontiers,
        to the opening of the Panama Canal,
the discovery of snail warfare in the margins
        of monastic manuscripts, the zero
that could hold an empty place, the neutron bomb,
        the seedless tangerine.
                                Some thought it
could be found in a dream of used-to-be—for Freud,
        it was his mama's knee; for Orpheus, Eurydice;
for Yeats, full moon that mixed its silver with
        the gold of Byzantium; for the *philosophes*—
time-whitened porticos of reason, poised high
        above the marketplace; for all the weary
workers, abundant Eden with its frolicking
        naked pair . . . oh, where *was* the fair
target to be found? this strange ground zero
        of desire, concentric circles, widening out
from a central lure, the jewel in the dragon's lair . . .

        But look! the weather vane is turning in
the wind—its arrow, *this* time, points the way.
        You can feel it in the air, beneficent and beckoning,
and look! a light that's bobbing up ahead, though
        strangely, it glows red, is swinging like a lantern
in the dark, the way trains used to look when they had
        passed, their smoke still hanging in the air, the light
                on their caboose a vanishing point of red.

MINE EYES HAVE SEEN THE GLORY OF . . .

I have watched you crank that sun up
in the morning, then drop it like the sand bag
that raises the curtain as the house lights fade;
I have seen you churn those waters up, then suck
them back, or stop them with a freezing wind,
monuments to their own motion, standing waves of ice,
polar bears stranded without a radio, seals
knocking their heads against the glass ceiling,
trying to rise. I have seen you eat the scenery
of a forest with a storm; raise a volcano
in a vacant lot, hot lava swallowing
the housing development; dry up the wetlands
just when the long-legged heron was eyeing a fish;
or, on the sunniest day—when the pastoral seems like
a documentary—loose a swarm of locusts
to devour the grain; set species against species,
roll the dice, two stars collide: time's assassin,
I have grown tired of keeping your accounts,
shaping a story from the chaos of your caprice,
the endless invention of your unconcern; I tire
of the argument, the contention, the attempt
to make a plot out of quicksand and fog,
to rouse the wind when becalmed, to comfort
the dead with a song:
$\qquad\qquad$ *ergo* I request reassignment,
a change of vocation, a more reasonable

situation: perhaps as a maker of kites—
something for the wind to take in passing,
the sweet unravel of string, line's pure extension,
revoking the "you," the merest invention—
a part of speech, the monologist's ersatz auditor,
gone with the kite, back, into airy nothing,
recalled: a local habitation, and a name.

TRACKING

for Carolyn Creedon

Yes, Carolyn, the ocean has its depths, its mezzanine,
the place between the blue, the green and those black waters
where the submarines feel their way by sound, the ear

the only guide when the lights grow dim, the place where
dawn has never reached, and there the giant Alba swims, ellipsis
of the deep, enormity, unseen, except on the sonar's

screen, bright shadow of leviathan or a merlin trick, for
at such a depth, such crushing pressures—it could not
live—and yet. The transitive exists, swimming the fissures,

like a recurring dream or a condor skimming the peaks,
as if Peru had been transposed below, or some great city sunk
and in its long, unlighted streets, finned giants slid along

the canyons of drowned tenements, and went their migrant way
through coral palings, kiosks hung with weed, falling ships
that spun like pearls in honey as they fell, while the great

Alba, scarcely a glimmer against the gloom,
swam on, its jaws wide, ingesting darkness like krill,
until it had swallowed all but its own glowing self,

and, tired of the conceit, shed its tons of matter,
rose in time to see first-light ignite the waves,
back in the blue delight of dawn, its ravishing *until*.

NOTES

The epigraph for the collection comes from a poem by Hayden Carruth, "Tartar" (in *Doctor Jazz*; Port Townsend, WA: Copper Canyon Press, 2001), whose setting is Hell, and whose speaker is "Timur the Lame" ("I killed / 300,000 people in my time, probably / more—"). He is among his friends down there:

> Bob Lee, Napoleon, N'Kruma, Alcibiades, Harry
> Truman, Charlemagne, all the great generals.
> We speak English and drink bourbon. Some killed
> more than I did, some less, but we did our best.

"*Wreck* and *rise above*": This title is the last line of a poem by Marsha Jansen in a *renshi* (poem chain) with her and Beverley Bie Brahic.

"In That Dawn": The title and the quoted epigraph are from William Wordsworth's 1805 *Prelude*, book 11, lines 108–9, and refer to his earlier intoxication with the ideals of the French Revolution.

"Thinking about Unamuno's *San Manuel Bueno, Mártir*": The three quoted lines in italics are, in order, by Emily Dickinson (from poem 254, Thomas Johnson edition), Muriel Rukeyser (from "Poem"), and Theodore Roethke (from "Fourth Meditation," part 2, in "Meditations of an Old Woman").

"Magnificat": The title is an ironic reference to the *Magnificat* or *Canticle of Mary*, Mary's praise to the power of God in the son she carries, from Luke 1:46–55, sung or recited as part of Christian liturgy.

"Saturday Night": The title was taken from the last line of a poem by Ann Stanford ("And say, sweetheart, you free this Saturday night?"), in a *renshi* with her and Marie Pavlicek-Wehrli.

"Voices from the Labyrinth": These poems had their origin in a request by book artist Enid Mark, with whom I had collaborated before, to write poems for a book she wanted to do on the theme of the Greek myth of the Labyrinth. She did not know, as we set out on this project, that she would herself be entering the labyrinth of hospitals and treatments, and would not live to complete the book. However, the art and layout were all but finished, and her husband, Eugene Mark, plans to bring it out as a posthumous limited edition from Elm Press.

I hope that the old story is still known: of the Minotaur, half man and half bull, love child of the Minoan queen and a bull, hidden away by King Minos in a labyrinth in the palace at Knossos, a maze cunningly devised by Daedalus; of the Greek Theseus who was sent as tribute from Athens to the powerful Minoan kingdom, and was meant for sacrifice; of Minos's daughter Ariadne who fell in love with Theseus, and gave him a clew (thread), which led him out of the labyrinth after he had killed the Minotaur. Theseus abandoned Ariadne on an island on his way back to Greece, where, because he had forgotten to change the black sails for white, his father, the old king, thinking his son dead, threw himself off the cliff into the sea.

But this is only the way Greek myth tells the story. We live a long way from there.

"Four Flats, Getting Dark Soon, Nothing to Do but Walk": As a tribute to the jazz composer Bob Zieff, the editors of the bilingual (Spanish/English) arts magazine *Sirena* asked poets from ten countries to respond to his jazz composition "Sad Walk." We were given a page of the score and a CD of four interpretations of the piece. And yes, there are four flats in the score.

I can't resist quoting something that Zieff said in that issue about his musical composition, because it expresses so exactly my experience of poetic composition: "My shaping of phrases is not pre-determined, but involves an adventure into the unknown. While most jazz, as with many other types of music, has ready-to-wear vertical sonorities (chords) my voices hold back or move ahead as they want—and some notes go where others might usually hold forth. In retrospect the less expected has it own inevitability."

"Encounter in the Local Pub": This poem owes its inspiration to the painting "Whiskey," by Chris Pelletiere, which can be seen on the cover of *Elegy with a Glass of Whiskey*, a book of poems by Crystal Bacon (Rochester, NY: BOA Editions, 2004).

"Restored to Blue": The epigraph comes from the poem "Sweet Nothing," by Christian Wiman in *Hard Night* (Port Townsend, WA: Copper Canyon, 2005).

"Trees, even at this distance": My title was borrowed from the title poem "Trees at This Distance," a new collection of poems by Marcia Pelletiere. It also owes to her something of the way, in the words of Roethke, "the spirit of wrath becomes the spirit of blessing."

"Harmony Bowl": The title comes from an item on the menu of the Laughing Seed Café in Asheville, North Carolina. I didn't order it.

"Headlong for That Fair Target": The title is from the last line of a poem by Elisabeth Lewis Corley as part of a *renshi* with her and Ginger Murchison.